THE CAPTIVATING, CREATIVE,

Unusual History of

Comic Books

BY JENNIFER M. BESEL

Consultant: Ethan Watrall
Assistant Professor
Departments of History and
Telecom, Information Studies, and Media
Michigan State University
East Lansing, Michigan

CAPSTONE PRESS
a capstone imprint

Velocity is published by Capstone Press,
151 Good Counsel Drive, P.O. Box 669, Mankato, Minnesota 56002.
www.capstonepub.com

Printed in the United States of America in Stevens Point, Wisconsin.
032010
005741WZF10

Library of Congress Cataloging-in-Publication Data
Besel, Jennifer M.
The captivating, creative, unusual history of comic books / by Jennifer M. Besel.
 p. cm.—(Velocity. Unusual histories)
Includes bibliographical references and index.
Summary: "Describes the history of comic books, featuring little-known facts and bizarre inside
information"—Provided by publisher.
ISBN 978-1-4296-4790-8 (library binding)
 1. Comic books, strips, etc.—Juvenile literature. 2. Graphic novels—Juvenile literature.
I. Title. II. Series.
PN6710.N63 2011
741.5'9—dc22   2010011665

Editorial Credits
Veronica Correia, designer; Wanda Winch, media researcher; Eric Manske, production specialist

Photo Credits
Alamy: Marmaduke St. John, 36-37; Capstone: 7 (all), 10 (left), 12 (all), 13 (top, bottom), 14, 15 (top),
17 (all), 22, 23 (all) 28, 29, 30, 31, 34, 38, 39, 40 (all), 41, 44 (top right, bottom), line art background
used throughout book); Corbis: Bettmann, 32; Courtesy of Jason Liebig, 35; Getty Images Inc.:
Bloomberg/Daniel Acker, 42-43, Buyenlarge, 8, Keystone/Alan Band, 44 (middle right); iStockphoto:
Seon Winn, cover, 5 (top right); Library of Congress: Prints and Photographs Division, 5 (bottom)
13 (middle), 44 (middle); Shutterstock: Agencia Box, 26 (left), antipathique, 16 (background), 18-19
(background), 22-23 (background, cloud puffs, exclamations used throughout book as design elements),
Bonita R. Cheshier, 40-41 (background), Christos Georghiou, 37 (superhero), 45 (top), Daisy Rano,
27(bottom), Danomyte, 4, 18 (bottom), 24 (right), 25, David Grigg, 21, Dawn Hudson, 33 (middle),
deedl, 26 (right), desaart, 27 (middle), Dietmar Hopfl, 44 (left), Dyonisos Design, 20 (top), Gary Paul
Lewis, cover (background) 6-7 (background), 38-39 (background), John Rawsterne, 33 (bottom), Julien
Tromeur, 9, 15 (bottom), Knumina, 33 (top), Montenegro, 9 (heart), Neptune, 24 (left), patrimonio
designs limited, 16, Rocket400 Studio, 32 (background), softRobot, 34, 38 (exclamations), Valentin
Agapov, 20-21 (blank book), Vertes Edmond Mihai, 27 (top), Willdidthis, 28-29 (background), Yelena
Panyukova, 26 (top); Tim Frady, 10 (right), 11; www.barnaclepress.com, 6

The author dedicates this book to her brother Steven,
whose comic genius will one day make him a superhero of epic proportions.

TABLE OF CONTENTS

Chapter 1

Origins

POW!

In a comic book, the graphics and story line work together to create an adventure you'll never forget. With the turn of a page, you can find yourself face-to-face with a world-famous superhero or a terrifying madman.

The world didn't always have superheroes protecting it, though. Comic books, as we know them today, developed over time. They started with simple black-and-white drawings that had a message.

BAM!

In the 1800s, black-and-white cartoon drawings became a popular way to make a statement. Thomas Nast became famous for his political cartoons that criticized dishonest politicians and slow government actions.

cartoon created by Thomas Nast in 1877

Artist R. F. Outcault took cartoons to the next level. Outcault created *Hogan's Alley*, the first newspaper comic strip, in 1895. Outcault used a single illustrated panel to tell a story. The strip's Yellow Kid character was extremely popular. The character never spoke. His messages were written on his shirt.

The Katzenjammer Kids by Rudolph Dirks came out two years after *Hogan's Alley*.

Early comic strips, like *The Katzenjammer Kids*, were made for adults.

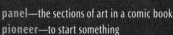

The Katzenjammer Kids was the first comic strip to use word balloons to note which character was speaking.

This strip also pioneered the use of several panels to tell a story.

panel—the sections of art in a comic book
pioneer—to start something

Comic strips quickly became a popular feature in Sunday newspapers. Some famous characters got their start in the funny pages.

Popeye debuted in the comic strip *Thimble Theater* in 1929. The character remains so well known that he's still used to sell cans of spinach!

Tarzan's comic strip debut was in 1929 in *Tarzan of the Apes*. But the character wasn't originally created for comics. Tarzan was pulled from the pages of a novel.

Dick Tracy debuted in 1931. Each week, Tracy fought against villains like Pruneface and The Brow. The villains were as ugly as their names sound.

The Phantom debuted in 1936. He was the first character to sport a skintight costume.

debut—a first showing

Chapter 2

Dazzling Debuts

Pulp magazines were popular in the 1920s. These illustrated magazines featured science fiction, adventure, and even romance stories. But they didn't use panels or word balloons.

Some science fiction pulp magazines featured stories about aliens.

In 1935, the worlds of black-and-white cartoons, comic strips, and pulp magazines collided. National Allied Publications published *New Fun* #1. This magazine included original story lines, narrative in word balloons, and several panels of art. **The comic book was born!**

narrative—a story

In 1938, National Allied Publications merged with another comics company called Detective Comics. They formed a company called National Comics. National Comics created some of the first superhero stories. Today, superheroes come in all shapes, sizes, and colors. But it seems that superheroes have some things in common.

Superheroes have extraordinary skills or powers, from superhuman strength to shooting lightning bolts.

A mask hides a hero's true identity. The Clock was the first comic book superhero to wear a mask.

Superheroes love their fellow citizens and always try to do what's right.

Skintight costumes are a must-have for many superheroes. However, modern characters Reuben Flagg and John Constantine have yet to give in to spandex.

The cape is the most recognizable hero accessory. Superman was the first hero to sport the flowing fabric.

9

THE HERO That Started It All

SUPERMAN IN 1940

In the beginning, Superman could not fly. But he could leap one-eighth of a mile.

SUPERMAN IN 1941

He soon gained the power to fly. Later he was also able to time travel.

After several years, the hero got X-ray vision.

In the early days, the comics said Superman could lift "tremendous weights."

The early Superman could run as fast as an express train.

FACT: A character named Steel Sterling was called the "man of steel" before Superman. But Sterling never became very popular.

In 1938, National Comics, which would later become DC Comics, was looking for ideas for a new comic book. Stuffed in a pile of other ideas was Superman. The idea had been turned down by many newspapers. But National Comics saw possibilities. They created *Action Comics*, introducing Superman, the first superhero ever!

Superman was created by Jerry Siegel and Joe Shuster. Siegel and Shuster had created other versions of the character. Their first Superman was a bald villain. Their second version made Superman a hero, but he didn't have any superpowers.

As his popularity grew, so did the hero's muscles.

SUPERMAN IN 1971

Over time, Superman's powers increased. He was able to run faster than a speeding bullet.

Notice how his costume has been updated over the years? Even with the changes, Superman is still the most recognizable superhero in the world.

Batman

Batman debuted in 1939. In original sketches of Batman, the hero wore a red suit and wings. But before the comic was published, his costume was changed. He got a darker outfit including a mask with pointed ears. In several early stories, Batman used a gun. But the character has since sworn off firearms.

Captain Marvel

In 1940, Captain Marvel jumped on the scene in *Whiz Comics* #2. For a while he was more popular than Superman. Originally, Captain Marvel was going to be Captain Thunder. But another comic used the name Thunder just before *Whiz Comics* came out.

FACT:
A spin-off called *Captain Marvel Jr.* was released in 1941. Elvis Presley was a big fan of this comic. It is said that he styled his hair to look like Captain Marvel Jr.

Captain America

Captain America debuted in January 1941. That was almost a year before the United States entered World War II (1939–1945). But the first cover of *Captain America Comics* showed the hero punching real-world villain Adolf Hitler.

Wonder Woman

Debuting in 1941, Wonder Woman was the first hugely successful female superhero. She was created by William Moulton Marston, who was also the inventor of a lie detection test. Wonder Woman carried her own lie detector—a magic lasso that forced people to tell the truth.

Spider-Man

Spider-Man, created by Stan Lee and Steve Ditko, first swung among skyscrapers in 1962. But Spider-Man was almost squashed on the drawing room floor. The publisher of Marvel Comics originally told Lee that nobody likes spiders.

Teaming Up

Not long after superheroes started saving the world, they began teaming up. In 1940, The Atom, Sandman, The Flash, and several others gathered as the Justice Society of America. Twenty years later, Superman, Batman, Wonder Woman, and several other heroes founded the Justice League of America. Eventually, the two teams even joined forces to fight bad guys.

The X-Men were a group of young people who were both classmates and superhero teammates. Each had special abilities and felt unwelcomed in the world. This story felt familiar to readers in the 1960s. During this time, people were working to end racial discrimination in the United States.

FACT: Stan Lee's original title for *The X-Men* series was Merry Mutants. Marvel changed the name, fearing people wouldn't know what a mutant was.

In 1983, Kevin Eastman and Peter Laird came up with the idea of a crime-fighting team of turtles. The next year they published 3,000 copies of *Teenage Mutant Ninja Turtles,* the black-and-white comic they'd created. Turtle mania exploded! The comic turned out to be a multi-million dollar idea. Soon everything from movies to toys featured the half-shelled heroes.

FACT:

In the United Kingdom, the team was known as Teenage Mutant Hero Turtles. Some people felt using the word "ninja" made the characters seem too violent.

SUPER HELPERS

Many superheroes have teamed up with sidekicks to defeat evil villains. After Robin the Boy Wonder joined Batman in 1940, other heroes recruited helpers. Soon Captain America had Bucky, Green Arrow had Speedy, and Sandman had Sandy the Golden Boy.

Some sidekicks were older than their partners. The Star-Spangled Kid's sidekick Stripesy was the adult of the pair. Green Lantern worked with a taxi driver named Doiby Dickles.

SUPERVILLAINS

Superheroes wouldn't have anyone to fight if there weren't supervillains.

Villains often grow into terrible monsters or wear frightening costumes. They usually have a name that reflects how they look and act.

Supervillains are often geniuses. They can develop elaborate plans and weapons.

These bad guys usually have incredible strength or tools that make them challenging opponents for superheroes.

Some villains want power and control, usually over the world. Others want revenge. Villains will do anything to get what they want.

FACT: The Thunderbolts were introduced as heroes in *The Incredible Hulk* #449 in 1997. Later that year, the Thunderbolts got their own comic. On the last page of the first issue, it was revealed they were really the Masters of Evil in disguise. This plot twist is considered to be one of the best in comic book history.

Villains are often as famous as the heroes who fight them. Magneto, Doctor Doom, and The Joker are considered three of the best villains of all time. Can you match these villains with the heroes they try to defeat?

MAGNETO

Magneto ranked number 1 on IGN Entertainment's Top 100 Comic Book Villains list. Magneto has the power to control magnetism.

FANTASTIC FOUR

The Fantastic Four is credited with changing the way comics treated superheroes. The members of the Fantastic Four were the first heroes shown with human feelings, fears, and troubles.

DOCTOR DOOM

Doctor Doom is a villain who can exchange minds with others. He is credited as being an inspiration for the *Star Wars* villain Darth Vader.

BATMAN

Batman is one of the most popular heroes of all time. Between 1966 and 2008, seven movies starred this superhero.

THE JOKER

The Joker uses practical jokes to try to gain power. The Joker was ranked number 8 on *Empire* magazine's list of Greatest Comic Book Characters in History.

X-MEN

In 1991, Marvel started one of its many X-Men spin-offs, called simply *X-Men*. *X-Men* #1 sold about 8 million copies. It is the best-selling comic book issue to date.

Famous Firsts

1939

First Super-Animal Appears

Rang-A-Tang the Wonder Dog fought spies and bad guys in *Blue Ribbon Comics*.

1940

Lex Luthor Debuts

Superman's greatest enemy, Lex Luthor, appears in *Action Comics* #23. In early issues, Luthor has a full head of red hair.

1940

First Female Superhero Debuts

The award for first female superhero goes to Fantomah, Mystery Woman of the Jungle.

1941

First Superhero Dies

The Comet is the first superhero to die in a comic book.

crossover—when characters from different comic books meet

1963

Iron Man Debuts

Iron Man's first appearance was in *Tales of Suspense* #39, written by Stan Lee. Iron Man wore a silver costume, not the red and yellow one we know today.

1965

Lobo Debuts

Lobo was the first African-American superhero to headline a comic book.

1974

Wolverine Meets The Incredible Hulk

Wolverine's first official appearance was in *The Incredible Hulk* #180, not in *The X-Men*.

1984

The Heroes Unite

Secret Wars, a 12-issue series, was the first company-wide crossover. The series brought together major Marvel heroes, including the Fantastic Four, X-Men, and Spider-Woman. Spider-Man's black suit was introduced in the series too, which would later be used for the villain Venom.

SAME NAME, DIFFERENT FACE

In the comic book universe, new characters can take on the name and powers of a hero who is no longer active. In 2004, an African-American character named Jason Rusch became Firestorm. He took over for the white man with that name who had been killed. The first two versions of Blue Beetle were white men. The newest version, which debuted in 2006, is a Hispanic teenager. The Crimson Avenger was originally a white man. In 2000, the character was reintroduced as an African-American woman.

Chapter 3

The Changing Face of Comics

Comic books, and the characters who live in them, have changed a lot over the years. The history of comics has been broken into time periods that explore these changes. Here's how things look in the history books.

PLATINUM AGE 1897–1937

Major Events:

- *Funnies on Parade* begins reprinting comic strips in a magazine.
- *New Fun* #1 is the first publication to use original stories and characters in a comic book format.

Major Characters:

- Yellow Kid
- Katzenjammer Kids
- Mutt and Jeff
- Little Nemo

GOLDEN AGE 1938–1955

Major Events:

- The superhero genre begins.
- After World War II, the popularity of superheroes begins to decline.
- True-crime, horror, romance, and Western comics gain popularity.
- The comic book industry adopts a Code for Comics in response to a movement against violent stories.

Major Characters:

- Superman
- Captain Marvel
- Captain America
- Wonder Woman
- Archie and Jughead

genre—a style of art

SILVER AGE 1956–1972

Major Events:

- Companies begin reusing old superheroes, but give them new stories, powers, and villains.
- Stan Lee and Jack Kirby team up. Together they create unforgettable characters and stories that strengthen the comic book industry.

Major Characters:

- X-Men
- The Flash
- Fantastic Four
- Hulk
- Spider-Man

BRONZE AGE 1973–1985

Major Events:

- Stan Lee and Jack Kirby end their partnership.
- Comic book stories become more mature, featuring real-world problems like drug abuse.
- Comic books that feature untraditional superheroes become popular.

Major Characters:

- Conan
- Swamp Thing
- Count Dracula
- Uncanny X-Men

MODERN AGE 1986–present

Major Events:

- Comic book characters become darker with many personal problems.
- **Independent** comics become popular, giving readers choices beyond DC and Marvel Comics.
- Graphic novels and manga become widely popular.

Major Characters:

- Watchmen
- Batman (reinvented as The Dark Knight)
- Wolverine
- The Punisher
- Spawn

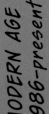

During the Golden Age of comics (1938–1955), superheroes were created by the hundreds. During the Silver Age and again in the Modern Age, heroes were adapted to fit the changing needs of their audiences.

historic cover showing
The Flash in the Silver Age

The Flash in the Golden Age

Secret Identity: Jay Garrick, a college student

Power: gained super speed by breathing hard-water vapors

The Flash in the Silver Age

Secret Identity: Barry Allen, a police scientist

Power: gained super speed when chemicals spilled on him. The chemicals had been on a shelf that was struck by lightning.

The Flash in the Modern Age

Secret Identity: Wally West. Before becoming The Flash, West was the crime fighter Kid Flash. Kid Flash also got his power by a chemical spill.

Power: As Kid Flash, the character already had super speed. When Barry Allen died, West took over the identity of The Flash.

TAKING A SWIPE AT IT

A swipe is a comic book drawing that looks like another on purpose. Often, artists will honor an earlier, often famous, cover or panel by copying it. Comic historians hunt through old comics, looking for swipes. One of the most swiped covers is from *The Fantastic Four* #1. More than 20 other comics have swiped that cover.

During the Silver and Bronze Ages of **mainstream** comic books, there was a rise in another type of paneled art. Large publishers, like DC and Marvel Comics, only published comics they believed would sell in large numbers. So artists began publishing work on their own. These books became known as underground comix.

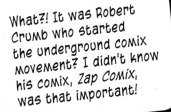

What?! It was Robert Crumb who started the underground comix movement? I didn't know his comix, *Zap Comix*, was that important!

Hold it! Dave Sim was pretty important to the comix and indie movements too. He wrote, drew, and published 300 issues of *Cerebus* himself. That's a record!

FACT: Robert Crumb sold his first issues of *Zap Comix* out of a baby carriage.

Underground comix didn't follow the mainstream publishers' Comics Code. The code limited what could be shown or talked about in a comic. Comix showed violence and drug use. Underground comix were definitely not for kids.

Indies

By the mid 1980s, comix were widely known for violent and drug-related story lines. Artists began to break away from that reputation. These new comics became known as indies or alternative comics. The stories covered all kinds of topics, except mainstream superhero stories.

I've figured out the secret to Jeff Smith's self-publishing success! His indie comic series, *Bone*, is one part dark fantasy and two parts humor.

Today, two companies have emerged as major players in the independent comics industry.

- Dark Horse Comics published hits like *The Mask* and Frank Miller's *Sin City*. Both of these were made into movies.

- Image Comics was founded by artists who had worked for DC and Marvel. At Image, the company doesn't own the characters it publishes. Writers and artists own the characters they create. Characters that Image has published include Spawn, Savage Dragon, and Witchblade.

MANGA MANIA

Manga is a Japanese form of comic book. Manga has been popular in Japan since the 1940s. But manga's big-eyed characters took a long time to become popular in the United States.

Manga is different from American comics in many ways. The biggest difference is that manga is read from right to left.

Some of the visual symbols manga uses are different from American comics too. For example, when a character is sleeping, manga doesn't show Zs coming from the mouth. Instead, a word balloon hangs out of the character's nose.

Lone Wolf and Cub by Kazuo Koike and Goseki Kojima is about a hired killer and his 3-year-old son. First published in 1970, it was the first manga work to become popular in the United States.

In the 1990s, anime, or Japanese cartoons, became popular. Shows like *Sailor Moon*, *Dragon Ball Z*, and *Pokémon* were huge hits. Kids flocked to buy anything with a Pokémon title, including the manga comics.

As sales of manga in the United States rose, sales of mainstream comics dropped. Today more manga comics are sold than regular comic books.

Manga stories cover fiction and nonfiction topics. In *Ranma ½*, the male character changes into a girl when splashed with water. *The Joy of Rice* by Tetsu Kariya is manga about Japanese food. There's a little something for everyone!

NOVELS GO GRAPHIC

Today the term "graphic novel" is used all the time. But in the 1970s, the term and the idea were just getting their start. Like manga, graphic novels changed the way people thought about the comic book art form. Both forms use panels of art. But instead of telling short stories over a series of comic books, a graphic novel tells one longer story.

art spiegelman

MAUS

Most graphic novels are printed and bound as books, rather than like magazines.

Graphic novels are sold in book stores, rather than on newsstands.

FACT:
Maus was the first comic work to win a Pulitzer Prize. The prize honors excellence in art and journalism.

A SURVIVOR'S TALE

I

MY FATHER BLEEDS HISTO

One of the most famous graphic novels is *Maus* by Art Spiegelman. *Maus* is a two-volume graphic autobiography. It focuses on the Spiegelman family's experience during and after the Holocaust. In the novels, Spiegelman shows Jews as mice and Nazis as cats.

art spiegelman

MAUS

Most comic books stretch a story across several issues. Graphic novels have a definite beginning, middle, and end in one book.

Graphic novels cover topics not usually found in comic books. Nonfiction and mature situations are popular topics.

A SURVIVOR'S TALE

AND HERE MY TROUBLES BEGAN

Chapter 4

Comics Controversy

If you think fights between heroes and villains are action-packed, just wait. Fights over copying, money, and morals are huge in comic book publishing.

JUNE, 1938

No. 1

ACTION COMICS

Superman vs. Captain Marvel

Action Comics #1 debuted in 1938 with a brand-new character called Superman. Two years later, *Whiz Comics* #2 debuted a superhero named Captain Marvel. That wouldn't have been a big deal except that the two characters were very similar.

Both characters are strong, muscular men with dark hair.

Both characters are reporters in their secret identities.

Both debut covers show the hero moving a car out of the way.

Both characters are caped superheroes, saving the day.

WHIZ COMICS

FAWCETT PUBLICATION

10¢

FEBRUARY · 1940

In 1941, Superman's publisher, National Comics, sued Captain Marvel's publisher, Fawcett. The legal battle lasted for 12 years. It only ended when Fawcett agreed to stop publishing Captain Marvel.

FACT:

Superman didn't fly in his story line until after Captain Marvel did.

SUPERMAN TIMES

Superman's Creators vs. Superman's Publisher
Siegel and Shuster Demand More Money

Jerry Siegel and Joe Shuster stand by sketches of the Superman character they created.

Siegel and Shuster spent 30 years trying to get back some of the rights. They lost lawsuits in 1947 and 1966. In 1975, DC Comics agreed to pay both men a yearly sum.

Shuster died in 1992, and Siegel died in 1996. The Siegel family believes DC owes them more money. The fight continues in the courts.

In the early days of comics, artists and writers often sold the rights to their characters. Publishers would buy the rights. That meant publishers owned the characters and any money made from using those characters.

Siegel and Shuster sold the Superman rights for $130. When Superman became a success, the publisher made millions of dollars. Siegel and Shuster didn't.

rights—ownership of and the power to use a work for profit

In the 1960s, Jack Kirby designed many famous Marvel Comics characters. In 2009, 15 years after Kirby's death, his family sent legal notices to Marvel. These notices state that Kirby's family should get ownership of the characters he created. If the Kirbys win in court, Marvel may have to stop using the characters Kirby created.

THE DYNAMIC DUO

Jacky Kirby and Stan Lee created some of the most famous characters of all time. Kirby was the artist. Lee was the writer. Here are just a few of their creations.

Black Panther	Iron Man
Doctor Doom	Magneto
Fantastic Four	Silver Surfer
Hulk	X-Men

…954, a book called *Seduction of the Innocent* by Fredric Wertham was …d. In his book, he accused crime, horror, and superhero comics of being …lent. Wertham said the comics caused young people to commit crimes. …m's ideas caused many parents to forbid their children to read comics.

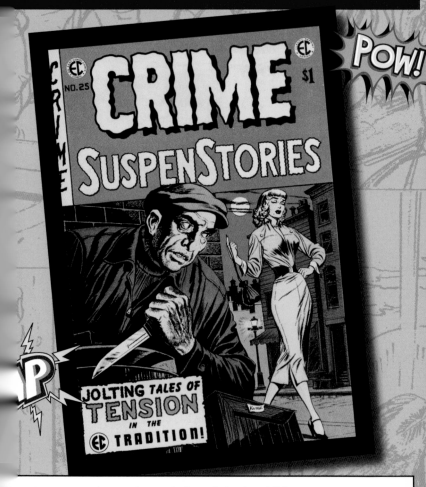

… U.S. government committee asked comic book publishers …nake their stories safer for children. The publishers …ated the Comics Code Authority (CCA). This group …de rules for comics and also an approval board. …he CCA approved a comic, its seal appeared …the cover. Most publishers agreed to follow …CCA's rules.

To Get The Comics Code Approval Seal:

All criminals must be punished.

Ads selling knives, fireworks, or tobacco are prohibited.

The word "crime" must never appear alone on a cover. If the word is used, it should not be larger than other words in the title.

APPROVED BY THE COMICS CODE AUTHORITY

Printed in U.S.A.

The words horror or terror must never be used in a title.

Use good grammar whenever possible.

Stories about vampires, ghosts, or werewolves are not allowed.

Over time, the public began to accept violence in the media. By the 1980s, few mainstream comic publishers still sought the approval of the CCA. And, of course, underground comix never tried to get the seal. Today the CCA rules are more relaxed. But only DC and Archie Comics still use the CCA.

media—communication forms that send out messages to large groups of people

Chapter 3

Comics and Our Culture

Comics have become a part of American and even world culture. Stories of famous superheroes are common knowledge. Comic book fans collect famous issues and gather to talk about their favorite characters.

In 1970, Shel Dorf organized an event in San Diego for comics fans to meet. It lasted three days and drew about 300 people. The tradition continued yearly. It became the biggest comic book convention in America. Today it's commonly known as San Diego Comic-Con.

Talk about true fans! Only one town in America shares the name of Clark Kent's city, Metropolis. In 1972, DC Comics allowed Metropolis, Illinois, to become the official "hometown of Superman." Every summer, the town hosts the Superman Celebration. Fans come from around the world.

FAN FILMS

Some fans don't just enjoy reading comic book stories. They also love making films based on their favorite characters. Fan films are independent movies that usually have an original story—created by the fan! They show their films online and at comic conventions. Some comic book companies allow this practice as long as the filmmakers don't make money on the projects.

Comic books take readers to fantastic fictional worlds. But that doesn't mean characters never tackle real-world situations.

In 1971, a story by Dennis O'Neil revealed that Green Arrow's partner was addicted to drugs. Speedy's superhero friends helped him beat his addiction.

Comic book characters die just like real people. But unlike in real life, most characters eventually return. However, in 1973, Peter Parker's girlfriend, Gwen Stacy, was killed—never to be brought back. This death had a major emotional impact on Spider-Man and Spider-Man readers.

COMICS FOR SALE

Comic book companies are not only creative in their stories. They are also creative in how they sell those stories.

In the 1990s, some publishers began printing certain comics with variant covers. The insides were the same, but the covers were different. Publishers were hoping fans would buy all the variants, earning them more money.

variant—a changed version compared to the main version

Another money-maker is for rival publishers to team up their characters. In 1976 DC Comics and Marvel Comics made a huge crossover. Superman and Spider-Man met—and fought—for the first time.

One of the oddest crossovers was *Archie Meets the Punisher*. In that crossover the squeaky clean teen meets the gun-toting Marvel **vigilante**.

Archie Andrews, an all-American teen character, debuted in 1941. Archie and his friends still run the halls of Riverdale High. The series has been going strong for more than 60 years.

The Punisher is called an antihero because he uses violence to fight crime. The Punisher debuted in 1974 in *The Amazing Spider-Man* #129. His mission was to kill Spider-Man.

FACT: Comic book series typically start with issue #1. However, some have instead started with #0. At times, a comic book series will start with #1 but put out a #0 later. Zero issues often tell a character's origin in a new way.

Various factors cause a comic book to become valuable. The debut issue of a popular character is worth quite a lot. An issue containing a key event can be worth considerably more than others too. You might want to check your attic for these valuable comics!

ALL STAR COMICS #58

debut of **POWER GIRL**

cost in 1976: $0.20

value today: **$80**

GRENDEL #1

debut of **GRENDEL**

cost in 1983: $1.50

value today: **$160**

THE AMAZING SPIDER-MAN #121

death of **GWEN STACY**

cost in 1973: $0.20

value today: **$800**

POLICE COMICS #1

debut of **PLASTIC MAN**

cost in 1941: $0.10

value today: *$10,000*

FLASH COMICS #1

debut of **THE FLASH** and **HAWKMAN**

cost in 1940: $0.10

value today: *$276,000*

DETECTIVE COMICS #27

debut of **BATMAN**

cost in 1938: $0.10

value today: *$1,075,500*

ACTION COMICS #1

debut of **SUPERMAN**

cost in 1938: $0.10

value today: *$1,500,000*

Many comic book characters have traveled from page to screen. In some cases, the silver screen made the characters more popular than they were in the comics.

Let's see if you know which characters made Hollywood history!

Match the question with the correct answer.

> 1. Who was the first superhero to be animated for movies?

> 2. Who was the first superhero to be featured in a **live-action** movie?

> 3. Who was the first superhero to have a prime-time TV show?

> 4. Who was the first superhero to star in a TV series of hour-long episodes?

Captain Marvel

Wonder Woman

Batman

Superman

ANSWERS:
1 - Superman 2 - Captain Marvel
3 - Batman 4 - Wonder Woman

live-action—featuring actors, not animation

Movies based on comic books are huge blockbusters at theaters. As of 2009, here are the highest-grossing comic book movies of all time.

MOVIE	YEAR	TOTAL AMOUNT MADE IN THEATERS
The Dark Knight	2008	$533,345,358
Spider-Man	2002	$403,706,375
Spider-Man 2	2004	$373,585,825
Spider-Man 3	2007	$336,530,303
Iron Man	2008	$318,412,101
Batman	1989	$251,188,924
Men in Black	1997	$250,690,539
X-Men: The Last Stand	2006	$234,362,462
X2: X-Men United	2003	$214,949,694
300	2007	$210,614,939

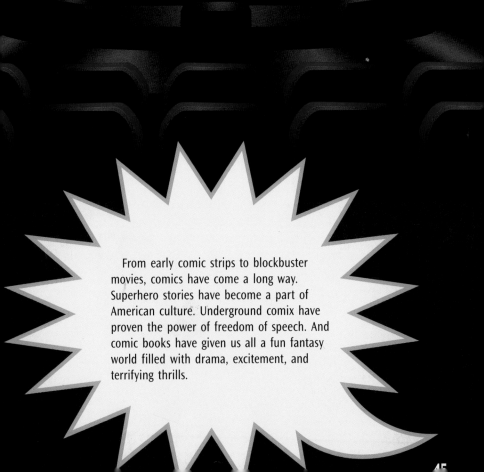

From early comic strips to blockbuster movies, comics have come a long way. Superhero stories have become a part of American culture. Underground comix have proven the power of freedom of speech. And comic books have given us all a fun fantasy world filled with drama, excitement, and terrifying thrills.

crossover (CROSS-oh-vuhr)—an instance where characters from different comic books meet

debut (DAY-byoo)—a first showing

genre (JON-ruh)—a category or style of art, music, or writing

independent (in-di-PEN-duhnt)—free from the control of a large company

live-action (LIYV-AK-shun)—featuring real actors, not animation

mainstream (MAYN-streem)—the most common direction or trend of a movement

media (MEE-dee-uh)—TV, radio, newspapers, comic books, and other communication forms that send out messages to large groups of people

narrative (NAR-uh-tive)—a story

panel (pan-UHL)—the sections of art and words in a comic book or graphic novel

pioneer (pye-uh-NEER)—to start something

rights (RITES)—ownership; the power to use a work for profit

variant (VARE-ee-uhnt)—a modified, adapted, or changed version compared to the main or standard version

vigilante (vi-juh-LAN-tee)—a person who works outside the law to bring justice

READ MORE

Krensky, Stephen. *Comic Book Century: The History of American Comic Books.* People's History. Minneapolis: Twenty-First Century Books, 2008.

Orr, Tamra. *Manga Artists.* Extreme Careers. New York: Rosen Pub., 2009.

Robson, Eddie. *Comic Books and Manga.* Crabtree Contact. New York: Crabtree, 2009.

Rosinsky, Natalie M. *Graphic Content! The Culture of Comic Books.* Pop Culture Revolutions. Mankato, Minn.: Compass Point Books, 2010.

INTERNET SITES

FactHound offers a safe, fun way to find Internet sites related to this book. All of the sites on FactHound have been researched by our staff.

Here's all you do:

Visit *www.facthound.com*

Type in this code: **9781429647908**

INDEX